Words

Of

Life

POEMS, SCRIPTURES AND PRAYERS

INSPIRED

BY GOD FOR LIFE'S SITUATIONS

LaKeisha M. Hall

THE
LEGNA
AGENCY

THIS IS A WRITTEN WORK BY LaKeisha M. Hall
PUBLISHED BY THE LEGNA AGENCY LLC

This is a book based on actual events and divinely inspired thoughts of the life of LaKeisha M. Hall. All content therein is written as recalled/recounted by her. All identities have been used by permission or/purposely omitted to protect the privacy of those living or dead.

WWW.LMHENTERPRISES.COM

WWW.THELEGNAAGENCY.COM

Library of Congress Cataloguing-In-Publication number **2011921957**

ISBN 978-0-9785104-8-0

First Edition Printing

Printed In the United States of America

AUGUST 2011

LMH Enterprises LLC
Post Office Box 481041
Los Angeles, CA 90048
213.538.8999

Dedication

First, I would like to thank and bless God for allowing me the opportunity to share his love through this inspired writing. Through trials and tribulations this book was able to be birthed.

In memory of my mother Sheila Conway, Grandmother Yvonne Watford and father William Thomas. The experiences that I have shared with each of you have given me strength to continue on living and to pursue after all that God has to offer and promised.

To my Aunties, Ms. Calin Fisher, Ms. Audrey Johnson, and Ms. Doris Cain thank you for the encouragement, words of wisdom, and your prayers and love.

To Minister Carla Robinson, Pastor Tasha Dawson "WOW!" is all that I can say when it comes to you mighty women of God. The love, the push, words of wisdom, and the beauty of my angels I say thank you.

To each and every one of you, who have contributed to my experiences I thank you for without those experiences this book would not have been possible.

CONTENTS

Dedication

Acknowledgments

Preface

ACKNOWLEDGMENTS

I would like to give special thanks to the following:

Bishop Blake and Apostle Harley

*To my wonderful and awesome publisher
Ms. Angel Holcomb and the LEGNA Agency, words
cannot express my sincere gratitude for you believing in
me and this book.*

*To my East and West coast family and friends you know
who you are thank you for the push!!!*

*To Mr. Clark thanks for having a sisters back through
the storm.*

*To all of the men and women of God that have prayed,
listened, preached, or taught… Thank You!*

*When, you can bypass the naysayers, remove the doubt
from your mind, and be obedient to God you discover an
awesome thing called "TRUST".*

Shalom,

Evangelist LaKeisha M. Hall

Introduction

Have you ever questioned what and why you are experiencing certain situation in life? Or, how should you handle these situations? If, so then *Words of Life* is the book for you!

Words of Life is a carefully created book that offers hope to those who are experiencing trails, tribulation, grief, rejection or loss of hope. Offering encouragement, strength, and uplifting words of divine inspiration, it is guaranteed to open up the well spring of hope to you that you may continue to face and embrace life one day and one poem at a time.

Evangelist LaKeisha Hall has experienced and survived grief as result of the deaths of her mother, father, grandmother and step-brother all within a sixteen month period and has conquered depression through the Word of God and her ability to convey her thoughts, feelings and emotions into this gem.

God began her inner healing through writing poetry and now Evangelist Hall passes these uniquely gifted words from God to you the reader.

Memorable, Captivating, Anointed! If I only had three words to describe this awesome work of God those would be it!

**Be Healed, Be Free, Be Delivered, Be Encouraged,
Be Strengthened & Blessed!**

Angel Holcomb
Founder & Senior Advisor
The LEGNA Agency
Creating A More Excellent Way! ™

Preface

When LaKeisha asked me to write the foreword for her new book *Words of Life*, my heart nearly burst! I can remember so clearly her early poem "***Breathe***" and thinking what a beautiful and passionate young woman she was. Now, many years later, as I read her published writings, I see her own heart has grown bigger, her dreams have become realized, and her words have bloomed triumphantly. This book is a most lovely gift, and I know readers will treasure it. LaKeisha, I wish for you a lifetime of love, luck, and continued success!

Fondly,
Professor Robyn Edelstein
General Education
Peirce College
Philadelphia, PA

Chapter One

Love

When you think of love what are you immediate thoughts? Do you equate love with the amount of gifts you receive? The amount of time you spend? How an individual treats you? Is it the respect, honesty, trust, and openness? Or, is it all of these above mentioned things and more?

As you read the poems in this *Love* section you will undoubtedly experience many of the above mentioned attributes. But, you also gain some wisdom as to what it is like to love unselfishly, be open to communicate, and to love someone with the love of God.

My experiences in this chapter truly have allowed me to grow in areas of my life that I never knew were possible. It challenged me to come out of my independent thinking, to forgive, to be healed, to truly love not just the person but myself even the more.

Love will require you to exam yourself, to explore your tolerance, to see if you are flexible, to evaluate who and what has been imparted into you. Yes, love truly does this and more. However, love should also give us wisdom to learn from our mistakes and mishaps.

Most importantly love should not leave us bitter though it may occur. I petition and plead with you to never allow your heart to grow cold and bitter. But allow true healing to come in from prayer, family and good friends.

Then be patient enough to wait, love yourself the more and love someone else. Love requires that you have an open heart, an open mind and don't allow fear to come into play.

A Love That Covers

Although, we can never explain the unexpected in life, we must remember there's a love that covers our hurt.

This love is unselfish, it's kind, it's humble, and it's never ending.

This love has no boundaries or limits on what to give back.

The only thing that's required is we give our hurts, faults, fears, and tears.

Tears we shed will cleanse the soul and rebuild the faith of knowing that there's a love that cares.

So, allow the love to cover and heal and know that God is always near.

Scripture Reading

Psalms 21:7 <small>AMP</small>

For the King trusts, relies on, and is confident in the Lord, and through the mercy and steadfast love of the Most High he will never be moved.

Prayer

Heavenly Father, I pray that when I'm not able to understand all that's going on in life and seem to be down, please remind me that there is a love that's unfailing. That unfailing love is yours. When everyone has gone his or her way, and nobody is around to lend a listening ear. I can always count on you God to be there. You're willing to love me even when I do not feel loved. Your love is always there God to comfort me in all storms.

In Jesus name Amen.

Companion

When, we think of companions we think of husbands and wives however, a companion is so much more.

You don't mind giving of your time, laughs, hugs, tears or/and fears because the companion is always near.

You have sought my face on how to care for your friend and because of this you have so much peace within.

I, thank you my child for being a companion to my servant for truly you have stood the test of time.

It's better than money, cars, and the finest of wines.

You are an example of a companion in human flesh.

My Spirit is so deep within you that every time you hear about Calvary, you bless Me because it was not you but Me.

That's not a bad thing at all because of man's great fall. He has sent me to redeem the price for man's iniquities.

So, you praise me for everything that I have done in your life because I your God did answer the call.

Just as I, God responded to the call for man's iniquities you responded to your call as that companion who, I am well pleased.

So, my companion continues to pray, sing, worship and study because all that you do exemplifies Me.

Scripture Reading

Hebrews 10:24 CEV

We should keep on encouraging each other to be thoughtful and to do helpful things.

Prayer

God, I pray that you would give me the heart, mind and spirit to encourage those who maybe going through. Allow me the ability to share love and kind words not only with loved ones but also to those who I do not yet know.

Let the words and deeds be done out of a pure heart and mind and not for recognition but only to bring a smile or hope to another life.

Let me remember when someone says a kind word or did a nice gesture and the experiences it brought to my life. We may never know exactly what that word may have done for that individual.

Help me to be aware of others and take the opportunity to encourage someone.

In Jesus name Amen.

He Cares

There's a man who loves me completely, a man who holds me at night and wipes away my fears. A man who reminds me of how sweet my youth has been to me.

A man who massages my heart when it, becomes too heavy from the burdens of life.

A man, who knows what every tear means when they fall from my eyes.

A man who came into my life when I was not even thinking about love.

The one who says, to me that you are beautiful even with the scars that are hidden within.

A man who says you are my QUEEN, who needs to raise up the young princess to become queens and the young princes to become kings.

Yes, this man loves me dearly for he carries all of my burdens that I was unable to bear.

Yes, a man I love so dear for God truly cares.

Scripture Reading

Luke 15:20 AMP

So he got and came to his (own) father. But while he was still a long way off, his father saw him and was moved with pity and tenderness (for him); and he ran and embraced him and kissed him (fervently).

Prayer

Lord, I pray when those days and emotions arise that I don't feel loved or appreciate that you touch my mind and heart letting me know you love me.

Sometimes, life throws many curve balls my way that I'm not sure exactly what to do. When that happens I will take a moment to pray to you. Knowing like a father you will open your ears and arms wide to embrace me.

Just like a father embraces their child when they see tears in their eyes or sense a little fear in their child, you will comfort me with your strength, word and love.

In Jesus name Amen.

I Need You

One soul alone unable to see the light, strolls in the darkness praying to God for a star.

In the mist of darkness, God sent a blinded soul that collides with another soul.

Both souls, at first were scared and not sure of their meeting.

God, allowed each soul to reflect upon others true emotions and meaning.

When, the two souls united the sky of darkness was now blossoming with light.

The souls needed one another to light the darkness that was in each of them.

I need you as the stars need the sky.

I need you as the seed needs water to grow.

I need you as you need me for love to blossom.

I need you for God has purposed us in the kingdom for his will and destiny to be accomplished.

Scripture Reading

Psalms 77:1 KJV
I cried unto God with my voice, even unto God
with my voice, and he gave ear unto me.

Prayer

Lord, when I'm in distress or in a joyful state
allow me to realize that I need you every step of
the way.

I will remind myself that I need you to provide
me with wisdom, knowledge and strength to
make in life complete.

I need you to instruct me on how to be a better
husband, wife, friend, sister, brother, employee
or employer.

I'm not perfect and I know that I have made
mistakes but I know that I can call on you and
you will hear my every cry.

In Jesus name Amen.

Personal Touch

When a soul has been bruised, ripped, and damaged, what is needed to repair it?

Is it, a soft word from a lover or friend who can deeply love the soul back? Or is it, an individual touch that does a quick fix?

How can the words or a touch mend a soul together?

Should, we allow such words or a touch to mend the soul?

Is, there one who possesses these unique qualities yet will still love and respect thee?

Yes, there is one who can do all this and more if we allow his perfect touch to heal and mend our soul.

A comforter, healer, provider and moreover He is that, our Lord.

Scripture Reading

Matthew 9:21 KJV

For she said within herself, If I may but touch his garment, I shall be whole.

Prayer

God, I pray to you for a personal touch on this _____ matter or situation.

I know that you are able to do all things.

God, you have touched me in other ways and I believe that you are going to touch me again.

Let, me continue to trust and believe that all things work for my good and not to be distressed but to have patience in this matter.

In Jesus name

Spiritual Parents

Who are spiritual parents? My mind and heart tells me that spiritual parents are those whom God gives as a precious gift.

God, gives us natural parents but what do you do when they have left to be in the glorious heavenly. You smile because God knows what he's about to do.

He loves me so dearly, that he did not neglect to leave me an inheritance. Yes, he provided me with loving spiritual beings.

A father, that's strong and stern as a rock. A mother, who is respected, loaded with wisdom and gentle as a flower.

Yes, we all have spiritual parents but have we tapped into the glory of the Lord for them to be revealing to us.

I bless God for He not only granted me natural parents but provided me with a second gift of special beings.

Yes, you are the spiritual parents I searched God for. Please know that you are loved and adored.

The trials that you two have gone through were meant for me to see how God brought you through.

So, spiritual parents let me thank you for taking the time to unveil wisdom, love, and respect to me.

Stay strong, focus on God and know that he has more spiritual children stopping by.

Scripture Reading

Proverbs 6:20-22 KJV

20My son, keep thy fathers commandment, and forsake not the laws of thy mother: 21Bind them continually upon thine heart, and tie them about thy neck. 22When thou goest, it shall lead thee; when thou sleepest, it shall keep thee; and when thou awakest, it shall talk with thee.

Prayer

Heavenly Father, I pray that you will send spiritual parents in my path that are willing to help me grow. Even, if I have biological parents I thank you for them as well.

I know that spiritual parents are needed to add another level of spiritual growth to my life. If, I have parents that are both physical and spiritual I am blessed.

However, if I have no biological parents then I'm grateful to the spiritual parents you have sent to let me know that I'm not alone.

In Jesus name Amen.

The Healing Oil

Many tears are shed for the desire of love never received, but God has covered us with His love.

God's love provides, shelter, strength and restores all His morning glory to one He adores.

The storms, which has built the characteristics to reform a generation of abuse.

The abuse could have been sexual, physical, emotional, and mental but God knows all.

It's God who provides the oil that will heal all wounds for His kings and queens.

Allow the oil to heal every wound because there is another generation that will need us to teach them about the characteristics of handling storms.

Scripture Reading

Isaiah 53:5 KJV

But he was wounded for our transgressions, he was bruised for our iniquities: the chastisement of our peace was upon him; and with his stripes we are healed.

Prayer

Heavenly Father, I pray for you to heal me in this area of_____.

The wounds from the actions and words still have an impact on me.

I want to be able to heal and to forgive so that I can move forward in my life. Even, if I never receive an apology from these individuals I need to be healed.

So, Father I thank you for hearing my prayer for healing and I believe that I will be healed from those experiences.

In Jesus name Amen.

Chapter Two

Encouragement

Often in life a time will come when we all need encouraging. The daily activities of life as a mother, father, daughter, son, student, professional, preacher, or your chosen field of work or passion can bring about stress, worries and uncertainness.

It's during these times that we may experience a friend, a loved one or a total stranger who will often words of encouragement. However, the ultimate person who needs to encourage us will be oneself.

The poems in the section where birth out during some of my most difficult pains in my life that no could really offer words of encouragement. For an example, when I experienced the death of my immediately family within a 16 month period. Or when I first moved to California I was homeless and jobless after 4 1/2 months of my arrival.

Words could not express the emotional drain or tiredness that my body however, I had to push and encourage myself daily that thing would truly get better. Through prayer and my faith in God and self-determination was I able to prevail.

So, to you the reader no matter what junction in life you may find yourself at right now, continue to encourage yourself. Continue to pray, read God's word and believe in yourself and you to shall overcome and you will!!!

Angel in the Mist

How my life has change so profoundly when an angel cross paths with me.

This angel has beauty and intellect yet has took the Lord's charge to help guided me.

When I have been in bondage, misunderstood, or not sure where to go, the Lord instructed the angel in the mist to go.

Yes, this angel has been visited by the Lord concerning me. Sometimes with firm words or a smile the angel has given me.

Who would have thought that in the latter part of my life that this angel would be a ray of light?

Often, I feel alone not sure where to go, this angel has offered a listening ear to listen to my woes.

Not being proud or selfish, this angel has put her best foot forward with her presences and finesse.

A mighty prayer warrior indeed, this angel is guided and filled with the Holy Spirit that the lord has anointed.

This angel has a distinctive ear from hearing from the Lord directly. Although, it's not often when this angel speaks, so when this angel open her mouth it's indeed worthy of listening.

So, my Angel in the mist what more can I say? But I hope this gift that God has given me to write will always encourage thee.

Although, it's a poem the Lord told me to write this to his angel as a usually song. There are more who will follow after me.

So, continue to stay in tune with the Lord for the other women and men paths you will soon come across to help indeed.

My Angel in the mist I thank thee.

21

Scripture Reading

Exodus 23:20 AMP

Behold, I send you an Angel before you to keep and guard you on the way and to bring you to the place I have prepared.

Prayer

Lord, I pray that you would send divine angels my way to help share wisdom, knowledge and understanding. Allow my heart and mind to be open to receive help.

Sometimes, this world can be cruel and even unfair but Lord give me the spirit to appreciate those you send my way to help. I know that I'm not perfect and I don't always have the answers.

However, when you send that angel to help me along this road in life let me be ready to embrace him. Help me, not to judge the outward man but allow me to see the person for the knowledge and experience that would help me succeed in this life.

In Jesus name Amen.

Faith

Although, sometime in life we never understand the plans God has for us but with faith we know that all things are possible.

We doubt if we're able to really achieve the things he has in store for me. The plans of prosperity, love, and patience surpass all boundaries.

Faith often has us walking alone no family or friends to call my own. Faith has us move to a different beat from other individuals we meet.

We would like to take everyone on this wonderful journey but the truth is everyone cannot attend. God ordained this faith for me to reach what he has placed high.

The highs are the blessings such health, strength, peace, joy and finances. However, it never what man can image.

Often, if we don't possess the big houses, cars or diamonds in man eyes we are failures.

Faith is only what we believe that God can do and allows us to achieve. So, even if you walk the journeys alone know that faith has never left your side.

For it's because of Faith that God is abiding inside.

Scripture Reading

2 Corinthians 5:7 KJV
(For we walk by faith, not by sight:)

Prayer

Heavenly Father, I ask You to guide me to walk by faith. There are some things that I may be fearful of. But I know that in order for dreams to come true I must first take a chance.

With the chance that I take I remind myself that it's the faith that allows me to take the chances in life that I choose to take.

No matter what the outcome maybe from the chances that I have embarked on. Allow me to gain wisdom and knowledge from the chance that led to an experience.

Heavenly, Father help me with any unbelief or doubt that I may have, faith in You and myself to take a leap of faith.

In Jesus name Amen.

Faith II

Often times I wonder how did I make it this far? With the many tears, fears and battles scars I have adhere from this world.

We, I mean I have failed myself so many times. Not caring if I live or die tomorrow.

When, the friends whom I was there for, was nowhere around when my turn came. No one came running but shut the door in my face.

I remember what a little bird once said...

"Just have faith!"

Have faith for what? My life seems hopeless and no wants to share now that they are in heavenly bliss.

So, when all seems to fail and no one around to care have faith because God is always there.

25

Scripture Reading

Hebrews 11:1 KJV

Now faith is the substance of things hoped for, the evidence of things not seen.

Prayer

God, I pray for faith to believe that dreams are possible to achieve. When I think that I'm not strong or when I'm not sure where to go allow me to believe.

Allow me to believe that all things are possible. When friends and family are not there give me the inner peace and strength to reach deep within myself to keep reach for my goals.

Help me, not to look at how long it may take or the many time I have to try but to keep believing in myself to reach for my goals. I will keep the vision in the front of the race.

No matter what obstacles or challenges may come my way I declare on this day that I will have faith to believe in myself to achieve all of my dreams.

In Jesus name Amen

Never Alone

Often when trials come our way, we feel there is nowhere to go.

We cry in the middle of darkness too afraid to show our pain or grief over what has occurred.

I feel as though all can understand such pain that I have endured.

But, there is one who speaks in the mist of darkness, saying you're never alone.

The voice, of a robin bird sing throughout the day reminds me that there is truly never so much pain.

At, the moment all I can feel is pain but, as I gaze into the sky and see the sun, listen to bird sing "Victory" you have already won.

So, when the pain seems so unbearable and no one individual is around just listen for the birds to sing that you are never alone for I have felt your pain.

Scripture Reading

John 16:33 NLT

I have told you all this so that you may have peace in me. Here on earth you will have many trials and sorrows. But take heart, because I have overcome the world.

Prayer

Heavenly father, I pray unto you that when the trials and tribulations of life comes my way and I'm not exactly sure what to do that I will pray to you.

I will pray for your peace to comfort me during the storms and give me strength to know that I'm able to go on.

Although, I might have to cry sometimes or even scream I'm reminded that I never alone because you Lord are always near to me.

So, I pray to you even now that I seek you for a word or listen to a song to can encourage me to go on.

In Jesus name Amen.

Push

Have you ever awoke one day and found that your world looks new?

Unable to comprehend the changes of life and not sure what to do?

You just push, push past the oppression and depression of life. See, there is more that you must see, hear, and touch to pursue your destiny.

Push, past the hurt and your own doubts of you cannot do this.

Do I have the strength to go on? Can I go on to finish this race of life?

Yes, you can finish this race but you must push past the faces. The faces of past lies, hurt, deceit, mistrust, and negative thoughts.

Just push pass, push down, push aside and push up because that's where you are going up to touch the sky.

Scripture Reading

Luke 5:18-20 KJV

[18]And, behold, men brought in a bed a man which was taken with a palsy: and they sought means to bring him in, and to lay him before him. [19]And when they could not find what way they might bring him in because of the multitude, they went upon the housetop, and let him down through the tiling with his couch into the midst before Jesus. [20]And when he saw their faith, he said unto him, Man, thy sins are forgiven thee.

Prayer

Heavenly Father, I pray that you may increase my faith in you that I may push past all hurts, doubts, and negative words that has affected me.

I ask for your strength to continue on believing that there is a better life awaiting me. To ensure, that I do not give up at this point in my life but to continue to push on and know that my present condition does not determine my end.

Give me the knowledge; wisdoms, and courage to push past anything that will try to hold me back from achieve my destiny.

In Jesus name Amen.

Trust

Who, in this world can I trust? Mothers are no longer nurturing or caring for their child because all they can care about are years and days of their youth when they had no cares.

Fathers are walking away from children because the world has become a place of no hope that anyone can imagine being there.

So, whom can I trust? Can I trust brothers' or sisters that no longer have love towards each other?

Whom can I trust?

I don't trust myself to keep my mind from breaking into scatter pieces.

Whom can I trust?

I can trust Jesus Chris because of what he did at Calvary for you and me.

I can trust Jesus because he shed his blood for me. I can trust Jesus because his life began 2000 years ago.

I can trust Jesus, he always there even when I'm at my low. I can trust Jesus because his word still outsells anything else that no history book can adhere.

I can trust Jesus because he's the only one who loves me enough who called my name and stop me from being in pain.

31

I can trust JESUS!!!!

Scripture Reading

Psalms 125:1 AMP
THOSE WHO trust in, lean on, and confidently hope in the Lord are like Mount Zion, which cannot be moved but abides and stands fast forever.

Prayer

Abba, I will trust you with everything in my life even the hidden things I might hide from others or even myself.

When, I not able to talk with anyone I know that I can talk and be honesty with you. For, you know every part of me.

So, allow me to be honest with you lord for I know that you will never turn your back on me. But, love me unconditionally.

In Jesus name Amen.

Uplift

Though, I walk on this journey of faith, sometimes my mind is in a constant race. I race within my mind wondering if my dreams are attainable or am I just dreaming away.

But, I remember what God said to me in his word and that is to just keep the faith.

Keep, the faith by lifting up my hands, my voice and my spirit so that it may dance with the Holy Spirit.

Uplift, my spirit to continue on the journey of life.

Uplift, my voice to speak and declare what God has promise me here in this land.

Uplift, my eyes so that I can see all the beauty that surrounds me.

Uplift, my head for when I lift my head, I have a sense to achieve what I imagine in my mind.

Uplift, my faith for when my faith is lifted up then the vision that God has given to me becomes more than a vision but a picture waiting to become reality.

Uplift, Uplift, Uplift, for there is life in you that must be birth into existence.

Scripture Reading

1 Peter 5:7 AMP

Casting the whole of your care [all your anxieties, all your worries, all your concerns, once and for all] on Him, for He cares for you affectionately and cares about you watchfully.

Prayer

Heavenly Father, I come to you with an honest and open spirit asking you for the ability to push forward all of the creativity that's lock up within me.

Grant me the clarity and wisdom to share the many gifts of beauty for the world to see and hear.

In spite of my shortcomings never allow fear or doubt to cloud my mind that I don't tried to push out the vision.

Lord, you proclaim in your word that I was wonderfully made in your image. Your, image is of kindness, generosity, love and compassion.

Let everything that my hands have been created to do reflect these exact characteristics of you.

I thank you in advance that gifts will uplift others individuals in the heart, mind, and spirit.

In Jesus name Amen.

Chapter Three

Freedom

The poems in this section depict the process of forgiveness, deliverance; healing and freedom for me.

Freedom and forgiveness can only start when you allow God to have his way in your heart and mind in becoming free.

When you allow yourself the opportunity to be free from hurt, anger and disappoints you become free from the bondage of your past. You will no longer view yourself as the victim but as victorious.

I have chosen to forgive and have freedom from my mother's drug addiction, my father betrayal of incest, my own indiscretions of looking for love in the wrong places and for those individuals that forsaken my kindness for their self-gratification.

To forgive and to be free opens up your lungs as to taking a new breathe on life. It allows you to grow, mature, and learn from life experiences. It provides that new confidence to go after dreams and to know that you are love and valuable.

I pray that these poems will help you to begin your own journey to healing, deliverance and forgiveness as well.

Beauty

My soul was lost and in a desert place of
no repair.

I wandered around the earth not able to see
the light in the mist of darkness.

Yet, you sent another soul in the same place
as me.

We, meet in darkness as two thunderbolts
and we touch and light was born.

Two, soul with similar paths come together
to embark only on one path.

One soul with a Pearle rib cage and the
other with a Crimson heart.

Soaring in the sky as beautiful Doves.

The beauty of Gods unity of the dark souls
into one Sunrise.

Scripture Reading

Romans 15:32 AMP

So that by God's will I may subsequently come to you with joy (with a happy heart) and be refreshed (by the interval of rest) in your company.

Prayer

Father, grant me the liberty to be able to allow another individual in my life to share my joys, sadness, ups, downs and my experience. For truly we all do need each other.

I pray that any hurts that may exist would be healed so that I'm able to be free. Free to encourage others, free to laugh, free to forgive, free to embrace and free to be me.

I ask that when individuals see me that they would see a very special unique and creative human being.

I pray that we would listen to one another, hear one another and most importantly respect one another.

In Jesus name Amen.

Freedom

*A*re the thoughts of freedom really keeping you in bondage?

Are you too afraid of what others opinion may affect the way you express the thoughts inside of you?

You must obtain the spirit of liberty thru the Lord, who died to set everyone free.

Be free, from the nightmares of the past. This includes abuse of every kind from verbal, sexually and indeed mentally.

Yes, drugs, pride, greed, jealousy, lust, and your own evil eyes.

Don't allow your low self-esteem to keep you bonded but allow and trust God to send his abounding and everlasting love.

Dear to be free, to enjoy what the entire world is awaiting to see.

Freedom, yes, it well worthy of achieving.

Scripture Reading

Colossians 1:13-14 AMP

[13] (The Father) has delivered and drawn us to Himself out of the control and the dominion of darkness and has transferred us into the kingdom of the Son of His love, [14] In Whom we have redemption through his blood, (which means) the forgiveness of our sins.

Prayer

Dear God, I pray that _____may be free in my/their mind, body, and soul to achieve all that life has to offer. Grant mercy and grace to my/their life and ensure them that no matter what has happen in the past that it's time to forgive and to be free to enjoy life.

Cause individuals to be able to see how much they are loved by family, friends and associates just being free of who they are. Create a spirit within them to be free from others opinion of who they should be. But to be all that you have created them to be in this earth.

In Jesus name Amen.

Good Bye

So many paths that started out in love ended with good byes.

The ones that united in one special night to create the human being, which is me. She born a daughter who turns around and born another daughter.

Here stands three generation of strong woman, who travel a unique journey.

The first, was born to a woman who fled the south and uprooted to the north to provide a better life for her children.

The second was a woman of strong will but fell victim to the world of drugs. Yet, she still remained strong to push the third woman to accomplish all that she could.

Now, the third is the one who has both of the two characteristics but has her own struggles to deal with. The struggle's of being the last one of her generation to embark on new grounds and to start a new legacy.

Yes, the third one will do like Christ and arise from the dead. She will sing like the daughters of Zion who awoke. This one will declare the Lord's Word.

Yet, as the third one embarks on the new journey she must say good-bye.

Good-bye to the pain of the last three years of her life. The pain of burying the first two, the pain of burying a love that she thought she found.

The pain of burying the old person who wanted to seek revenge but remember what the Lord her God said, "Vengeance is mine."

So, to all who have sustained hurt, pain, guilt and anger remember, it's time to say good-bye. For God, has something more special in mind for you.

Good-bye to all that tried to stop me including myself. Good morning O daughters and sons of the most High King. Arise!!!

Scripture Reading

Isaiah 60:1 KJV
Arise, shine; for thy light is come, and the glory of the LORD is risen upon thee.

Prayer

Heavenly Father, there will come a time in my life when I must say good-bye. Good bye to relationships that may cause harm. Good bye to jobs that are no longer fulfilling, good byes to old cities and states but when the time comes give me the strength to say goodbye.

All good byes are not bad but must be done to start a new chapter in one's life. And when my time comes to say good bye give me the courage and confidence to do it.

Let, no fear or regrets stand in my path but allow a peace to be within me as I start a new journey.

In Jesus name Amen.

It Is Finished

The bonds of love was filled when God breathe on you two. Created a being like a rose in a desert

The river of life from the creator breathe on me now, the bonds has been lifted in the sky and has never kiss the rose good bye.

On April 10, 2006 the bonds fell off, releasing the "ROSE" to blossom into the world.

Remember, the bonds were from God. It is finished and the rose must say goodbye.

The "ROSE" will now populate the world with seeds to flourish.

Now for God, has the bonded with the Rose.

Scripture Reading

Ecclesiastes 3:1 KJV
To everything there is a season, and a time to every purpose under the heaven:

Prayer

Father, I pray that when it is time for something to come to an end give me the strength and heart to accept it.

Although, I might not want to release some things or say good-bye I know that nothing always last forever.

Even when it doesn't make sense allow me to know that all things happen for a reason and that a lesson will come from all experience.

I might hurt for say good-bye but provide me with strength, courage and healing to move on. I might have to cry a few times but I know with you God everything will be all right.

In Jesus name Amen.

New Song

Sing a new song of life. Are you willing to sing to a different beat other than what life has dealt?

A new song of joy, peace, and liberty it's not in a thought that the song forms.

The songs have been awaken in you to sing take the chance and just sing.

A new song, yes the song that has been singing for years. Open up your spirit and just sing it's been waiting in you to ring out loud.

Yes, the new songs that will change your history, destiny so just sing out loud.

Scripture Reading

Isaiah 12:5 *KJV*

Sing unto the LORD; for he hath done excellent things: this is known in all the earth.

Prayer

Lord. I pray that you will grant me a new song for my life every day that I'm able to awake.

Rather, it's sunny or raining outside because you allow me to take another breathe I will sing a new song.

Even, when life may seem hard I will sing a new song because I have the power to either allow things to affect me in a positive or negative way.

So, Lord I pray and thank you for the ability to see great things even if it's present in a negative way.

In Jesus name Amen.

Praise

I am a vessel that is wonderful made. Although, there were some bumps, bruising and tears I still have a praises.

There are times in my life, were I felt rejected by the one who were supposed to love me.

Sometimes, my family was my very enemies. Enemies, because of the shade my skin, my hair, and my laugh as to lack of what they thought I should have.

Yet, I came to myself, I realize there was no mistake on what I' am because I was wonderful made.

Even, with my bumps and bruise in my life I still have a praises.

I have a praises because I made it another day.

Scripture Reading

Psalms 116:1-2 KJV

[1]*I Love the LORD, because he hath heard my voice and my supplications. [2] Because he hath inclined his ear unto me, therefore will I call upon him as long as I live.*

Prayer

Abba, help me to praise you in the good and the bad times. I can give praise when all things are working out find but when times are not so smooth is when I need to talk with you.

Help, me not to neglect given you praise every day. Rather it's with a song in the shower or a moment of meditation in the car; just allow me to give you praise.

I praise you even now for having breath to breathe and the ability to see.

In Jesus name Amen.

Tears

Tears are good for cleansing the soul.

Tears are sometimes a dew of what heaven is like.

Tears, gives us an insight to the power of healing within. Tears, brings comfort for the broken hearted to mend.

Tears show some that you though you never exists that you do.

Tears, brings out the very essentials of you.

Tears are God gift to us to show all types of emotions. Tears, we should all shed for is helps make room for the new and improve you.

Don't be afraid or too proud to shed tears for it opens you up to receive more information about who are growing into.

Scripture Reading

3 John 2 KJV

Beloved, I wish above all things that thou mayest prosper and be in health, even as thy soul prospereth.

Prayer

Father, I pray that when it's time to shed tears that I will not let pride stand in my way.

Sometimes, I may not want to cry because it can be a sign of weakness but let me know that tears are need to help cleans the soul.

Lord, when I need to cry because of hurt or happiness let me do so. Let me show my emotions because that lets me know that I able to feel compassion for others.

In Jesus name Amen.

t h

Chapter Four

Purpose

I often had these wonderful and great ideas that I could see manifesting but somehow only a few actually were birthed. You see I allow other opinions of what I should do influence what God had given me.

Unable, to really grasp the ideal of doing great and awesome things sometimes put fear in me. If, we could all be truthful we have allowed doubt and fear to stop us from progress forward in some areas of our life.

This book has been one of my biggest fear. I was not sure if individuals really want to read what God had placed in my heart to give or even if I was that good of a writer.

One day after going in line for prayer the preacher ask me "Why are you crying so hard? What has you?" I reply, God has given me this book to write and to be honest I'm afraid of success. The preacher reply: If, God has given unto you he will truly see it come to pass and accomplish all that it suppose do.

A few years went passed and I realize that I was being my worst enemy. Sometimes when we don't have the entire pieces to the puzzle we become paralyze and don't walk in faith. We believe we must have everything place but that's not always the case.

Purpose is defined in the Webster's Dictionary as something one intends to get or do. However, if we never take those first steps how will we know where the steps it will lead? In anything you peruse it will take risk, faith, and possible some failure but the key is to continue.

These poems represent many points in my life when I had to stop being my worst enemy and seeing how God sees me. Encouraging myself to continue on even when it does look like anything is blossoming.

As, Bishop Charles E. Blake has once said in a sermon: If, God has given you a though, vision, or dream act upon it. As, I LaKeisha Hall say: "Take a leap of faith for you never know where you might land.

A Servant

Oh, my chosen vessel how I'm pleased with thee. You have learned to suffer in peace and not complain about the injustice you sometime had to bear.

You see, all that you experience was not a waste on your behalf but you allowed me to form you into my work piece.

My humble and obedient servant you are, when I look at you it's as the stars are dancing bright in from of me.

Because you have not taken the praise or the glory for what's been done.

No, you have turned it around and gave it back to me. Oh my chosen vessel how I'm pleased with thee.

I have seen you fall and pick yourself back up again, upon my grace instead of running to hid you continue to run on here in this race.

As my word has declared one day we will be face to face.

So, my servant how please am I with thee, as you continue to offer up praise, glory, and majesty to me.

My servant, my precious son of rare wisdom, strength and courage don't you see oh how proud I am of thee.

My servant, my servant, my servant, continue to dance with me.

Scripture Reading

Matthew 24:46-47 KJV

⁴⁶Blessed is the servant, whom his lord
when he cometh shall find so doing.
⁴⁷Verily I say unto you, That he shall make
him ruler over all his goods.

Prayer

Heavenly Father, I pray that you will grant
me the heart of humbleness to work with
confidence, strength, boldness and trust.

Whether, my position is an employer, an
employee, a wife, a husband, a brother, a
sister, a pastor or teacher. Allow me to
take pride in my work that it may have a
positive outlook to effect anyone that I may
come into contact with.

Let the work you assign to my hands
influence others to be better a persons as
well so that we can impact the world.

In Jesus name Amen.

Chosen

The years that you have sown in tears were shed for the knitting of paths prepared by me.

The paths, which many are not able to bear Yet, I looked down on you from the moment you were formed. Yes, he is the one I will adorn.

I will adorn them with the strength, wisdom, and endurance to weather the storms. My storms are to form the characteristics of me.

Yes, the one who died at Calvary. They pierce me in my side from on high the blood flowed. As the flow of the blood the anointing flowed onto you.

You must teach and preach for there are souls that need to be secured and freed.

To fly to their destiny, I have set in place for you are the one I have chosen to release souls sent by my grace.

So my sons and daughters in this year of manifestations, look up because that's where I'll be.

For your endurance, stands, and cries I' am now lifting you on HIGH.

Scripture Reading

Jeremiah 1:5 AMP

Before I formed you in the womb I knew (and) approved of you (as My chosen instrument), and before you were born I separated and set you apart, consecrating you; [and] I appointed you as a prophet to the nations.

Prayer

Lord, I come to you asking what my purpose maybe in this life? I'm not sure exactly what to do and sometimes I just don't feel capable of doing anything.

Lord, please allow me to remember that I was chosen with a purpose to do something in this life. Help me to know that I don't have to copy from anyone but can just be myself and use the gifts that you have given to me.

Help me, to surround myself with positive individuals and remind myself that I was chosen for a purpose. No matter how big or small allow me to follow my dreams and be the best at what I would like to achieve.

Lord, I thank you for reminding me that I am some special and that I have been chosen to do great things.

In Jesus name Amen.

Fragrance

As my eyes swell with tears, I remember how you felt that day.

The day the nails went through your flesh.

I sit here now wondering, why you would go through so much pain for a sheep like me?

Now, as I feel your pain from others as I walk on the path you have design for me.

I, remember the love shown at Calvary. So, I will go through the pain for your name.

I, remember you are the "SHEILD" that covers me with Dews of rainbows and fragrance of love.

I will keep looking up because you have shown love.

Scripture Reading

1 Peter 4:10 CEV

Each of you has been blessed with one of God's many wonderful gifts to be used in the service of others. So use your gift well.

Prayer

God, allow me to be able to share my gift that you have given me to help others smile and to bring peace to their life.

Provide me with opportunities that this gift can be seen so that I'm able to give you praise for what you have provide.

God, let the gift provide love, trust, friendship and business opportunities. Opportunities to help others grow and to be inspire.

Let me arise each day smelling a new fragrance of creative with my gifts to help my family, friends and community to use their gifts as well.

Let the gifts of us all create a beautiful world for each other to see.

In Jesus name Amen.

Obey

Like a child scorned by a caring parent who's loving and understanding God is the same.

He's the father who has chosen his children. He seeks, teaches, answers and loves us so dear.

What will you do?

Do you run from your calling and possible jeopardize the purpose that God has placed you here on earth to do?

Or, do you accept the calling and enjoy the journey, which is good in all ways.

The trials, tribulations, crying, and smiling is being obedient to the fathers voices that inside of you.

Be obedient to impact this world for the gifts and talent that has been grace upon you.

Scripture Reading

Proverbs 4:1 AMP

HEAR, MY sons, the instructions of a father, and pay attention in order to gain and to know intelligent discernment, comprehension, and interpretation (of spiritual matters).

Prayer

Lord, I pray that you will give me peace to obey the inner voice that speaks within me.

Although, others might not understand my decisions at time allow me to have faith in you.

Give me the strength to obey and to take a leap of faith towards my dreams and goals in this life.

Lord, when I'm scared or not exactly sure of what to do allow me to take a minute to pray to you for guidance.

In Jesus name Amen.

Thank You

Often in life, God send someone your way to encourage you with words like "keep the faith".

Keep on believing, keep on achieving, keep on hoping and never give up.

Know that God is activating a master plan. A plan for you to impact someone's life by bringing a shining light of hope that shines ever so bright.

So, I say thank you for your smiles, hugs and laughter. Because of these wonderful qualities you possess I realize that my life really does matter.

Not, that my life did not matter before but through the storms that I have faced, God has allowed your wonderful qualities to impact my space.

Thank You

Scripture Reading

Hebrews 10:25 CEV

Some people have gotten out of the habit of meeting for worship, but we must not do that. We should keep on encouraging each other, especially since you know that the day of the Lord's coming is getting closer.

Prayer

Abba, I asked that you never allow me to forget human kindness when someone has been kind, helpful, or courtesy towards me.

Never, let the cares of the world or my life be so consume that I'm no longer in touch with being kind towards someone else.

I pray that my mind will be open just like yours Abba to care for others and not to be judgmental toward any individual because of race, gender, or religion.

Give me your Spirit of love for all your creations.

In Jesus name Amen.

Total Recovery

Truth of God

Obedience to God

Trust in God

Available to be use by God

Loyal to God

Restoration of God's love

Excellence in God spirit

Courage from God

Obligation to do God will

Victories in God

Evangelize about God

Reverence God spirit

Yield to God voice

Scripture Reading

1 Peter 5:6-7 KJV

⁶Humble yourselves therefore under the mighty hand of God, that he may exalt you in due time: ⁷Casting all your care upon him; for he careth for you.

Prayer

God, I pray unto you that I will be still and wait on you for the change in my life.

Right, now I feel uncomfortable and not able to comprehend my next move so I will just trust in you for total recovery.

Recovery, from past disappointments, mistakes and hurts but I wait on you to give me the strength to persevere.

For, I cast all of my care on you to move on behalf for total recovery in my life.

In Jesus name Amen.

Uncertainties

What do you do when you have planned things and they don't fall through?

Do you lay your head down and wonder why or what did I do to deserve this much strife?

Do you crawl away, not answering your phone and hope to die?

Meaning, to give up on the dreams that God has given you in the inside.

Do you call on the name of God? Do you pray or do just allow the tears to flow from your eyes?

Well, with uncertainties of losing a job, a love one, or friend there will come a peace that wells up from the inside out.

It's the peace of knowing you will survive the uncertainties of life because God has equipped each of us to strive to reach our destiny, which God has built from the inside out.

That destiny or dream maybe writing a book, becoming a cook, a teacher, a preacher, a dancer, or a producer, a loving mother or a caring father.

But know that these steps of uncertainties all work together to unlock our dreams and destiny

Scripture Reading

Hebrews 10:35-36 KJV

[35] Cast not away therefore your confidence, which hath great recompense of reward. [36] For ye have need of patience, that, after ye have done the will of God, ye might receive the promise.

Prayer

Heavenly Father, I pray to you right now for strength. There are many uncertainties that I'm facing at this moment in time and all I can do is call on you.

I call to you for I know that you can hear my prayers and I believe and trust that you would provide the answer for me.

I will not move in hast but will wait patiently for you to provide that correct guidance for my situation.

Allow me to wait with strength and courage for a wonderful outcome.

In Jesus name Amen.

Chapter Five

Life

You will be amazing to know that the poems in the Life chapter were not birthed out because my life was great but in fact the other way around.   The fact of the matter is that I was going through more grief and sorrow for any one human being.

Actually, I was attending college and I had already experienced two deaths within two months of each other. One death was of my brother and the other my father. It was not until 10 months when my grandmother died writing start for me.

My English professor Mrs. Edelstein, had given an assignment to the class where everyone had to write a poem. My very first poem entitled "Breathe" was what the Lord gave me in remembrance of my grandmother.

After my professor read the poem she suggested that I have the poem published.   However, I thought they were just mere words and did not react at that moment in time.   All of the poems in this section were written during many ordeals and trials.

However, I want each of you to know just because storms come your way does not mean you give up. Instead, it's a mean for you to begin living life better and wiser. Never, let life choke the life out of you but just begin to breathe again.

Breathe

My throat was as a thunder storm moving
though heaven and hell of life.

My soul has seen glory and grief; the tender
years of a grandmother hand holds my face.

The echoes of abuse, addictions and lies a child
looks into the summer souls.

Hell snatches my entire heaven away. Tears
almost taste like sweet melons; the bitterness
reminds me of respect.

Sing, the songs of Zion in the aisle for the
solider has marched to the melody of grace.

Holding, my face and seeing fear and fury
increase the love and diminishes the cries.

Breath once more oozes the strengths guiding the
grieving angel to answer destiny.

Seated by the angel arches a touch tells the angel
to begin breathing and breathe again.

What I did not know, what I did not know?

The breathing began and prayers were now
singing.

69

Scripture Reading

2 Corinthians 1:3-4 KJV

3Blessed be God, even the Father of our Lord
Jesus Christ the Father of mercies, and the God
of all comfort; 4Who comforteth us in all our
tribulation, that we may be able to comfort them
which are in any trouble, by the comfort
wherewith we ourselves are comforted of God.

Prayer

Heavenly Father, I pray for strength in my life at
this moment in time when all things seems to be
going wrong.

I pray that my pain would soon turn to joy and
that I would be able to laugh and smile again after
all the tears are gone.

It's seems like no one is around to comfort me at
this moment in time but I know that because of you
that I will make it through.

It may not be today or tomorrow but I know that I
will not always be in this state of mind. So, I ask
you God for peace at this moment in time. To be
able to go on another second, minute, hour, and
day.

In Jesus name Amen.

Field of Lily's

The winds blow across my face as I awake from a dream.

As I dream, about me running across a field full of Lillie's. The Lillie's were different colors of the rainbow.

Each color symbolizing something different in me, the Red was for all of the pain I went through.

The Yellow reminded me there was still hope waiting for me.

The Black were days I was not able to comprehend my thoughts.

The Blue to remind me of the water that washes away everything negative thing.

The White for the purity of the rebirthing of a new me, the fields of lilies was my story being told by the spirit lifting me to go on. That is the spirit of God.

Scripture Reading

Isaiah 43:18-19 CEV

[18]Forget what happened long ago! Don't think about the past. [19]I am creating something new. There it is! Do you see it? I have put roads in deserts, streams in thirsty lands.

Prayer

Lord, I pray that anything from the past that is not helpful or beneficial to me in this present day in time please help me leave it all behind.

I don't want to look in the past but want to concentrate on the future. Sometimes my mind may wander back to pass events but give me the hope to continue to move forward.

Lord, sometimes it may be hard or even a little sad that I must leave others behind but I must go forth to accomplish the goals that you have planned.

In the process of moving toward my accomplishments send me to be kind to those who you send to help me. Allow no pride to take place but to remain positive, humble and hopeful in pursuing happiness, love and grace.

In Jesus name Amen.

I Believe

I believe that my breath begins when I believe in myself.

Believe that my soul awakens when I love myself. Believe that your life is good when you don't have the strength to go on.

I believe each sunrise speaks to my soul to believe that I'm an eagle in the sky.

I believe that when my wings open up to fly the morning dew from the sky is a refreshing to my heart to beat again.

I believe, that the moon when it shines reminds me to believe that my life is filled with purpose by design.

I believe, I believe, I believe that my light is shining again.

I believe.

Scripture Reading

Judges 20:22 AMP

But the people, the men of Israel, took courage and strengthened themselves and again set their battle line in the same place where they formed it the first day.

Prayer

Father, when doubt seems to arise in my heart, spirit or mind give me the strength to believe the opposite for my life.

Allow me to run to your word and search it out and let it take hold to my spirit to believe in things and myself that I'm able to accomplish.

Let, the doubt and fear fall to the waist side so that I'm able to climb whatever mountain maybe in my way.

I will encourage myself with positive words, thoughts and songs to help me along to move forward into my purpose.

In Jesus name Amen.

Live

*L*ive again just as Jesus called Lazarus from the grave. I must be called from the dead.

Begin to breathe into my soul and begin to breath God's breathe.

Began to sing songs of life, for there is still life to be lived.

Begin to wipe away every tear, so that you are able to see everything clear.

Begin to hear from God again, for instructions to endure this life once again.

Begin to never stop trusting God at His Word, for He knows how things should end.

Begin to live yet life again, live, live, and again still live.

Scripture Reading

1 Corinthians 7:17 AMP

Only, let each one [seek to conduct himself and regulate his affairs so as to] lead the life which the Lord has allotted and imparted to him and to which God has invited and summoned him. This is my order in all the churches.

Prayer

God, I call unto you to hear my cries and to let me know that I have everything to live for.

I might not think or even feel like I have anything to live for at this moment but I know that I do.

I speak to myself at this moment saying that I must live because I need to go further in life.

I must live because I have not seen my dreams come true yet. I must live because I love myself and I know that I'm precious to God for he has created me.

I again say to myself in Jesus name that I must live.

In Jesus name Amen.

Restoration

My heart was broken in so many places that I was not able to see the many tricks sent by the enemy.

He planned from the moment I was born to rob, steal, and kill what you had pre-destined for me to achieve.

I embark on this life with my own set of plans, one that including sailing the sea, flying in the air, and enjoying life without to many burdens to bear.

Who, would have known that the trials and tribulation was for something more powerful than I could have ever image.

The tears and scars from emotional, spiritual, and physical abuse from those who were to protect me.

Little, did I know that it was all for this life like yours at Calvary. Then, one day you made an emergency call to my mind, spirit and emotions.

You said, it's me your father from on high calling you into a place that will help others be free.

I was there when these things took place.

Some of your own doing and some from others who did not know your place in me.

Don't be angry with those who did not know who you are. This was done for restoration has begun. Now,

you are restored and you shall restore those back to me.

Scripture Reading

Psalms 55:16-18 KJV

¹⁶As for me, I will call upon God; and the LORD shall save me. ¹⁷Evening, and morning, and at noon, will I pray, and cry aloud: and he shall hear my voice. ¹⁸He hath delivered my soul in peace from the battle that was against me: for there were many with me.

Prayer

Father, I pray for the moment to be restored again. I have gone through many trials and tribulations and don't feel whole.

But, with the assurance of you love that I can be restore again. Restore me better than what I was before.

Provide a more positive attitude and outlook on life with greater tools of understanding from my life experiences.

In Jesus name Amen.

The Heart

The heart what a precious instrument made by our heavenly father. An instrument yet small and fragile but beat strong when in love, pain or peace.

The heart is small as a fist yet strong as marble, the heart, what a tender instrument that's flows out life.

Yes, the heart when taken care of is so overwhelmed with joy and happiness that money can't buy.

However, when the heart has been shatter and not able to heal itself, there's one thing that can mend it back.

The heart is Jesus' way of reminding me, you, we, and us that he has our heart and can mend and heal any broken pieces.

Scripture Reading

Proverbs 4:23 AMP

Keep and guard your heart with all vigilance and above all that you guard, for out of it flows the springs of life.

Prayer

Lord, provide me with the wisdom to guard my heart in all situations. Allow me to seek for instructions, wisdoms and knowledge for making all decisions.

Keep me grounded so that I'm able to allow my heart to be open to receive encouragement and love. But don't allow only my heart to make decisions.

Lord you have provided me with wisdom so let me use that as well. If, my heart happen to be hurt by someone else or of my own doing allow me the time to heal.

Heal, so that I can once again be able to receive and release.

In Jesus name Amen.

I Need You

One soul alone unable to see the light, strolls in the darkness praying to God for a star.

In the mist of darkness, God sent a blinded soul that collides with the other soul.

Both souls, at first were scared and not sure of their meeting.

God, allowed each soul to reflect the other true emotions.

When, the two souls united the sky of darkness was now blossoming with light.

The souls needed one another to light the darkness that was in each of them.

I need you as the stars need the sky.

I need you as the seed need water to grow.

I need you as you need me for love to blossom.

I need you for God has purpose us into the kingdom for his will and destiny to be achieve.

Scripture Reading

Psalms 77:1 KJV

I cried unto God with my voice, even unto God with my voice; and he gave ear unto me.

Prayer

Lord, when I'm in distress or in a joyful state allow me to realize that I need you every step of the way.

I will remind myself that I need you to provide me with wisdom, knowledge and strength to make in life.

I need you to instruct me on how to be a better husband, wife, friends, sister, brother, employee or an employer.

I'm not perfect and I know that I have made mistake but I know that I can call unto you and you will hear my ever cry.

In Jesus name Amen.

Chapter Six

Men

In my life I have come across all types of men some good and some not so good but in each of these individuals they all had the ability to possess and achieve great things in life. Some of these men I have known for years and others are some that I meet and had a brief conversation with.

Many of men are struggling from past mistakes that society, family members and even you are fighting with yourself to forgive and to let go.

When, I see men and how they were created in the very image of God my heart aches for them to achieve all that life has to offer. The birthing of these poems are to encourage all the men of the world to want more and to go after their dreams and visions.

I encourage you my royal priesthood, kings, and prince to be strong in the mist of this economic crisis. Continue to hold your head up high and know that you have been created in God imagine and when God created you he said that it was good.

Believe and encourage yourself to do well. If, no other individual believes that you can achieve... I do! Know that you have all of the tools and equipment necessary to be successful not by man's opinion but by God's.

Please don't expect everything to go easy but apply yourself and do the work for it will pay off greatly. Most importantly keep your faith in God and yourself. When, you hit a stumbling block keep moving for your sister is cheering you on.

A Father's Strength

Is a father someone who biological helps fertilizes a woman seed into a human being?

Or is it someone who has the strength and humility to help other grow into the best they can be?

A father strength, are those men who were once boys and have now grown into men.

Grown men, who are not afraid to share life struggles, glory, and pain. They teach with their actions, words, and courage.

They show young boys how to grow into men and young girls into women.

They are our brothers, husbands, co-workers, bosses, doctors, lawyers, authors, postal workers, teachers, coaches, pastors, barbers and our next door neighbor.

So, for all of the men who have shown strength, faith, tears, laughter, and a tender heart thank for you for showing a father's strength and love.

Scripture Reading

Deuteronomy 32:11 CEV

The Lord was like an eagle teaching its young to fly, always ready to swoop down and catch them on its back.

Prayer

Lord, I pray for the men of the world and ask that you will strengthen them to be all that you have called them to be. Give them the mindset to encourage and inspire other men to achieve greatness.

Lord, for the men who are not the natural father of a child but who maybe a mentor I ask that you grant them the ability to teach others. Not being ashamed to share their stories with others to possible help stir someone clear of past mistakes.

I ask that the receiver will take an understanding and knowledge to help impact another young man or men lives. May this affect the community, homes, businesses, churches and other entities of men for a more productive life.

In Jesus name Amen.

Man of Valor

O man of valor is thee who are clothed with spirit, knowledge, and integrity.

Despite, what society has tried to dictate to thee, you have been thru storms, floods, and hard winds that have blown but stand tall because it shows how much you have grown.

Man of Valor, wear humility well and continue to broaden your horizon for your not able to tell just how far you will go.

Remember, to keep God alive in you and pray often for he will see you thru.

Man of Valor, let this just be the beginning of your walk of faith, strength, joy, peace, and most of all your CHARACTER for other men to become Men of Valor.

Scripture Reading

Genesis 5:1-2 NIV

[1]This is the written account of Adam's family line.

When God created mankind, he made them in the likeness of God. [2]He created them male and female and blessed them. And he named them "Mankind"[a] when they were created.

Prayer

Father as a young man/man I know that I don't always do right. With all of the pressure of the world it just hard sometimes.

But God I pray that I will not use that as an excuse not to become the man that I need to be.

I will become the might man of valor for myself for I must achieve great things in this life.

Father, help me to tap into my spirit and pull out all of the gifts that you have given to me. No matter what my age might be I know there is still time for me to accomplish my dreams.

I will believe in myself to become that great man you intend for me.

In Jesus name Amen.

My Kings

Oh my sons, where have you gone?

I look for you day and night yet my search has returned back
void.

I need you my sons, for there is so much to do. I have
ordained order yet it starts with you.

My men, I need you, for you are the pillar for my woman and
children.

I'm given you instructions that will carry you into your
destiny.

I know, it seems that you have been suffering but I have deep
need of you to become more than just part of society.

You, have great purpose locked in you that I need to unlock
for an appointed time to fulfill the destiny.

Life, yes life, has been hard but I'm only picking a handful to
achieve the instructions I have set before thee.

So, lift up your head up high, the chastisements, the rebukes,
and the corrections I have sent forth because I know what's
locked up in thee.

Please, be obedient, respectful towards each of thee. For,
these are important components to unlock my destiny.

My men, I love you my precious Kings.

Scripture Reading

1 Peter 2:9 CEV

But you are God's chosen and special people. You are a group of royal priests and holy nation. God has brought you out of darkness into his marvelous light. Now you must tell all the wonderful things that he has done.

Prayer

Father, I pray that as I take on this journey called life that you will equip me with the characteristics of a king.

Meaning to be loyalty, honesty, humbleness confidence, strength, wisdom and being able to learn from others.

Lord, allow me to know that I'm not able to do it all myself so give me the heart and spirit to allows others to teach me as well.

Allow me to receive knowledge and wisdom from other individuals to help me grow into the king that you have called me to be.

In Jesus name Amen.

Pillars

Pillars, are strong they give support to hold up or to carry the loads that sometimes are too heavy for others to do alone.

When, I see man, I see man as the instruments that God created you to be. Pillars, no matter what you face in this tough world sometime turns God beauty into a discrepancies.

See, men you are pillars that were born to shoulder the burdens of one another, each other, and others to see and follow in this journey of life.

Don't you see? Men please become what God created you to be. Even, with past mistakes don't allow that to be your crutch for not getting back into the world and continue in the race.

No matter what was said or done remember you are one of God's best creations on the face of the earth. So, my pillars please get back up.

There are many who need, want, deserve and desire for many pillars to come forth.

So, pillars of this earth take your positions and seek God for your earthly assignments and move forward in his kingdom business.

Scripture Reading

Psalms 18:32 NKJV

It is God who arms me with strength, And makes my way perfect.

Prayer

Heavenly father it is you that said in your word that you have cloth me with strengthen to endure. So, I come before thee asking for your strength of today.

*You said in **Proverbs 27:1** Do not boast about tomorrow, For you do not know what a day may bring forth. (NKJV) Only you God know the beginnings and ends of the day.*

Strengthen your man servant to be built up by your words. Help me to have integrity, humility, respect, honesty and trustworthiness. Increase my knowledge and wisdom to do great things here upon earth.

Allow, my heart to stay pure and to in tune with your spirit as I become a mighty pillar to help others as well as myself to be better and to achieve goals.

Lord, I pray that you will send other pillars my way so that we may be united and help young men and young women become mighty pillars.

In Jesus name Amen

Rise Up

Rise up my mighty men of strength, character, and honor and take your rightful place upon this earth.

Rise up to teach, lead and bring forth knowledge in this earth that would resurrect the dry bones of mankind.

Rise up my brothers, fathers, uncles, nephews, leaders, preachers, and sons for God has command and commission you to do a great work.

Do to the best of your ability but always rely on the one who created you. You see God created you in his image for his purpose and his plan.

But, don't allow the negative effects of this world to release you from his command. He has commanded you to produce out of the creative gifts that he has bestowed upon you.

You men were meant to be Kings, Princes, and a Royal priesthood. Just like Abraham, Elijah, Moses, Jeremiah, Ezekiel, and Isaiah speak forth the words in which you were created to do.

Rise up, Rise up, Rise up and my mighty men continue to rise up.

Scripture Reading

Matthew 7:24 AMP

So everyone who hears these words of Mine and acts upon them [obeying them] will be like a sensible (prudent, practical, wise) man who built his house upon the rock.

Prayer

God I come to you asking for your Holy Spirit to fall and indwell upon me. I need you God more than anything to become the man of God that you have ordained me to be.

Let anything that's not worthy or causing me not to grow in a positive way be remove from my thoughts, spirit, and heart. God, I ask that you create in me a clean heart healed from all past hurt and mistake.

You and only you are able to do this. I speak words of life over my life to grow, move, invest, create and be free to enjoy the beauty of this earth. I speak over not only my life but those who have connected to me to be successful as well.

Thank you, God for raising me up out of any trouble, problem or circumstance that are too heavy for me to handle. And, even for the one that I'm able to handle provide with your wisdom on how to react. Let every action, spoke word and deed come from you.

In Jesus name Amen.

Royal Priest

My men you have been given the power and authority to walk and speak as the royal priesthood I command thee.

I've provided you with instructions and guidelines how to operate, innovate and generate here on earth.

But you must submit and tap into source of life that lies within you to be awake.

My royal kinsmen of the most high proclaim with a loud voice and screams of worship to invoke the heavenly sky.

How, I truly love my royal princes and have provided you the ability to take control to rule from the kingdom of grace.

Stand and position yourself for a great blessing to flow your way my royal priesthood are you truly ready to commit and obey?

For, it's through your obedience to submit that these blessings will truly flow so please don't be afraid to let of you ego.

There's no need for arrogance, pride or greed for you are God seed, a seed that was created to grow.

So, I say once again to my royal priesthood let the world truly see how the Lord and Savior truly rest inside of you indeed.

Scripture Reading

1 Peter 2:9-10 MSG

9-10 But you are the ones chosen by God, chosen for the high calling of priestly work, chosen to be a holy people, God's instruments to do his work and speak out for him, to tell others of the night-and-day difference he made for you- from nothing to something, from rejected to accepted.

Prayer

Heavenly Father I pray unto you on this day to grant me the courage, wisdom and strength to accomplish any dream, vision, and though you have provided.

Help me to overcome every fear that may arise during my journey. Allow me never to be ashamed to call and cry out to you for help. Give me the humility to talk with other men that I may gain knowledge to go forward.

Inspire me, also to give wisdom and encourage to other men who may need guidance as well. Let me be a light that will transform other individual's life to do great things.

In Jesus name Amen.

. *My Voice*

Lord, I have a voice to speak up and out for the things that I believe in a mighty voice that can impact a neighborhood, a city, a state and even a country such as the United States.

My voice carries power to deject all negative that can cause harm to me and those in my unity. My voice carries power to project positively that can elevate the human spirit.

You see I have a choice on the words that I speak and what comes to life through me.

I chose to speak life and not death and just like Martin Luther King there is a dream living inside of me.

My brothers we all have dreams screaming to break forth and to launch us into our God given destiny.

So, men let us use our voice to change the course of the legacy we want leave in America history.

Scripture Reading

Proverbs 18:21 NLT

The tongue can bring death or life; those who love to talk
will reap the consequences.

Prayer

Father, provide me with the wisdom to guard my lips
before I speak. For, I know that I have power to either
speak life or death and I want to speak life.

Even, when someone may have wrong me help me come to
you and pray. I know that this will not always be easy
to do but father please guide me in all that I should do.

You have given me a voice to do great and might things
to better this world instead of the decaying this world.
So, again I ask not only do you direct and guide my path
on this journey in life but also guide my mouth on what
to say.

In Jesus name Amen.

Chapter 7

Women

When, I look over my life and think of the many women who had a hand in raising me from a baby into a grown woman I can truly say I'm blessed. Although, some of these same very women have experienced some tremulous trials they continue to persevere.

Not many of these women were family but they are woman who I have meet in college, co-workers, bosses, church members, first ladies, friends and just some strangers that I had the pleasure of talking with.

See, to look at me from the outside you would have never imagine some of the heartache and dilemmas I face. Some of the dilemmas were so bad I was not sure if I could arise to a new day and continue on.

It was because of my English Professor Mrs. Edelstein, who recommended my very first poem entitled "Breathe" to be published that I thought of writing. It was also not a time when I could see the light in the mist of the darkness. However, six years later what once started as one poem has become a book.

When I think of the many women of the bible and the trials they face it should serve as a notice to every young girl, young lady, and woman that we have everything going for us. My grandmother use to have a saying "what don't kill you will only make you better and stronger."

Think about it, God created us from the strongest part of man the rib cage. When you think of the rib cage and what it protects that she provide women with an insight on how strong we are. The rib cage protects the very essentials organs that helps maintain life. The heart is protected, the lungs are protected, and the kidneys are protected all by the rib cage

Not only that the female living creatures are only creature that can carry life. So, we have been destiny to bring forth life in every situation that given to us. We are the Esther, Ruth, Deborah, Naomi, Rachel, and the Proverb 31 virtuous woman.

So, no matter the test or the trials, woman you been created to birth out new possibilities from old tragedies and new beginnings that no one has ever imagined. Stand tall my beautiful queens and walk with your head held high and do not ever mummer I cannot when truly you can do.

A Love Letter from God to His Women

My Daughters don't fret the trials you have been going through. Being single, married, divorce, or a widow these are my choices for you.

I have to groom you from the inside out. I must heal the wounds that many are suffering from now. Some are so deep that it will take years of surgery.

Yet, my daughters let me operate for the plans I have for you are great.

See, if you can love me while you're in the mist of the storm the one I will send will surely adorn you. For he has searched me to reach you and he knows the plans I have for you.

He will treat you as a queen loving, respecting and fulfilling my needs. I will give him divine instructions on how to minister to you.

First, let me be your everything even after I bring you your king. Don't forget me your first love the one who slept with you. The Who held you in the midnight hours washing away your fears. The one who held you as the tears flowed.

I'm your everything before you every thought of a king. Remember, I AM the King who will be there for you even when you're going through.

So, my daughters remember daddy loves you. I'm only taking you thru the storm to perfect you.

When you are finish going thru you will continue to love me your Father, the Lord and King give me all of the praises for your Destiny.

Scripture Reading

Isaiah 54:10 KJV
For the mountains shall depart, and the hills be removed; but my kindness shall not depart from thee, neither shall the covenant of peace be removed, saith the LORD that hath mercy on thee.

Prayer

Dear God, I pray for _____ please allow her to see just how wonderful, beautiful, and intelligent she is. Let her know that you have created her with all intentions for her to succeed in life.

No matter the hurt or pain she is able to heal and continue to move forward in life. God, show her your undying love even when she may feel alone or lonely with no one to talk to.

Let, her know that all she has to do is pray unto you and you are always there willing to listen to her every cry without judgment but with love.

In Jesus name Amen.

A Mother's Love

A mother is someone who's willing to share a love that's unconditional; it touches you in a place that you only dream about.

A mother's love is directly sent from God above. He gives this special gift to those he entrusts to exemplified him.

This love, shares in the good, bad, and ugly. It's a love that offers words of encouragement, hope, strength and wisdom.

A love that covers, cares, comforts and offers an open ear to listen.

Yes, a mother's love is so tender and caring that when you think on a mother's loves it warms the soul and reminds us to continue moving on in life to fulfill dreams and destiny.

A mother's love is not just a women who born a child, but it's an Aunt, Niece, Sister, Cousin, Co-worker or just a wonderful Woman.

A woman, who exhibits this inner beauty and quality, is truly from the Lord as a gift to be treasured.

Scripture Reading

Proverbs 31:10 AMP

*A capable, intelligent, and virtuous woman--
who is he who can find her? She is far more
precious than jewels, and her value is far above
rubies or pearls.*

Prayer

*Lord, for every mother that's not sure if she able
to raise her child alone or with a spouse I pray
that she will remember that she has the
capability to raise a child.*

*Lord, allow her to see that she was chosen for a
wonderful opportunity teach, show, and impart
knowledge into this child life.*

*For women who take on the role as a mother
through friendship, sisters, aunts, and cousin
please be encourage for the lord has given you a
great opportunity as well to show a mothers
love.*

*God, I pray for their strength to continue on
loving, sharing, and communicating.*

In Jesus name Amen.

A Love Letter from God to Married Women

Oh virtuous woman of Zion, how I love thee so much. I created you from Adams rib to be a helpmeet and yes the backbone too.

With you I took special time to create, making you just like the finest and the rarest of wine. I know that the mate I made for you sometime have you lying awake at night. But please remember I made you perfect to be his wife.

Not, all the time does the man understand all of my plans. But my special married woman this ministry is part of your destiny.

Remember, you have to pray, meditated, and lay prostrated before me in order for me to give you divine instruction on my plans for both of thee.

Yes, I made man in my image for them to walk upright and tall, yet you are the soft vessel I made to borne. That means to give life to the thoughts and plans that I have given man.

I know sometime it seems life is not fair, remember I your Father, Lord and King has great things in store for thee.

So, my married women of God lift your head up high. I have given you a great deal of responsibility but I knew you would accomplish the task for you follow after me.

So my precious ruby more worthy than any stone, I count it an honor that you my daughter have not taking this ministry lightly and thrown in the towel. Remember, you already wear a crown.

A crown that only was created by me with love, laughter, and smile from above. Your father is watching and is very proud; keep looking up for me because my hand will be always reaching down.

Scripture Reading

Isaiah 54:10 KJV

*For the mountains shall depart, and the hills be removed;
but my kindness shall not depart from thee, neither shall
the covenant of my peace be removed, saith the LORD
that hath mercy on thee.*

Prayer

*Dear God, I pray for_____ please allow her to
see just how wonderful, beautiful, and intelligent she is.
Let her know that you have created her with all
intentions for her to succeed in life.*

*No matter the hurt or pain she is able to heal and
continue to move forward in life. God, show her your
undying love even when she may feel alone or lonely with
no one to talk to.*

*Let, her know that all she has to do is pray unto you and
you are always there willing to listen to her every cry
without judgment but with love.*

In Jesus name Amen.

Woman of Wisdom

A *woman of wisdom exemplifies beauty and strength. She is kind hearted, intelligent and full of zest. She gives herself to all who would take heed to gleam from her.*

She knows how to be gracious even in storms and never allows a challenge to pull her down why because she has the strength that God has given her.

Yes, this woman of wisdom is unique and special designed as a rare jewel. So, on this day I celebrate this wonderful, powerful, beautiful woman of wisdom which is you.

Scripture Reading

Proverbs 7:4 AMP

Say to skillful and godly Wisdom, You are my sister, and regard understanding or insight as your intimate friend--

Prayer

Lord, I come to you asking that you allow you love, thoughtfulness, and Holy Spirit to fill me today. I pray that every decision that I make it made with true and godly wisdom.

Help me so that when others may come to me for advice that if any advice is given is of your spirit and not my own. Keep me before thee for prayer and for guidance every day.

Whenever, I'm not able understand or perceive things correct grant me the ability to maintain my peace so that I will not hurt or offend anyone. I thank you in advance for the wisdom that will come out me to assist others in Jesus name.

In Jesus name Amen.

Special Ladies

Although it might be hard at this present time please don't forget to allow your tears to be shed to help cleanse the pain away.

Take this moment of opportunity to grown stronger in your faith and in your spirit. Like a seed that has been planted waiting for a rose to bloom.

My special ladies listen to the heart beat of God and stay in tune.

My ladies, be encourage by this experience to grow in grace for only selection of woman can endure the journey of life sometimes called a race.

Keep believing, keep trusting and keep moving forward, for if you don't give up you are sure to come out with more knowledge then before.

So, my special ladies look up high to the sky and mountains around, for your feet have been planted firm and sure to arise like the morning sun.

Scripture Reading

Psalms 139:13-16 MSG

13-16 *Oh yes, you shaped me first inside, then out; you formed me in my mother's womb.*

I thank you, High God—you're breathtaking!
Body and soul, I am marvelously made!
I worship in adoration—what a creation!
You know me inside and out, you know every bone in my body;
You know exactly how I was made, bit by bit, how I was sculpted from nothing into something.
Like an open book, you watched me grow from conception to birth;
all the stages of my life were spread out before you,
The days of my life all prepared before I'd even lived one day.

Prayer

Abba, I asks that you keep_____ full of your love at this moment in time. Where she may feel weak and tired give her the strength to endure.

Allow, her to know that she's wonderful and beautifully made and that there's no mistake for her life. Ensure her God that you have gifted her with talents to share with the word because she special to you and others.

Let her thoughts about herself be good and send other ladies and men that will encourage her along her journey in life. Never allow past mistake to stop her from moving forward.

Abba, send your warmth and love to her in the midnight hours when there may not be anyone around and speak the promises for her life this night. Abba, I thank you now for what will be produced in the special lady life. In Jesus name Amen.

A Woman's Strength

A woman was created by God from man; she was made from the best part of man the rib.

The rib cage protects the lungs, protects the heart, it protects the liver the very essential parts that allows us to function as human beings.

A woman's strength is her character, it's her beauty, it's her honor, and it's her respect.

Who is this woman of strength? She is one who has endured, she is one who has cried, she is one that has sought the very face of God.

She is the one who has uplift, she has encouraged, and she is the one who breathes life into all existence.

She is our mothers, our daughters, our sisters, our aunts, our girlfriends and our nieces.

She is one that will walk with her head held high when the clouds are around.

She is one that walks in grace through the storms of fire.

She is one that sits tall even when the world is on her shoulders.

She is a woman of strength. This woman of strength is within each of us.

We must tap into what God has placed and created in us which is a woman of strength.

So, my women seek the Lord and ask him to reveal all you are supposed to do here on this earth.

Continue to educate, evaluate, uplift, grow and change for a true woman of strength never runs one leg of the race.

Scripture Reading

Psalms 18:2 AMP

The Lord is my Rock, my Fortress, and my Deliverer; my God, my keen and firm Strength in Whom I will trust and take refuge, my Shield, and the Horn of my salvation, my High Tower.

Prayer

Abba, I pray unto you that you will teach and bring forth the very essential character of being a woman of strength. There are time in my life when are the chips seem to be down but never allow me to forget that you created me to be a women of strength.

Show me through your Word and prayer the right ways to handle this world and the cares of life. Allow me to be humble enough to cry and to seek additional help when it just seems too much for me to endure.

Abba, you are truly my source and strength and help me to never forget that you created me a wonderful, talented, and blessed human being.

In Jesus name Amen.

Inspire

To inspire someone is to release of oneself the wisdom,
Love, and generosity to another..

To inspire gives one the hope and enlighten for a better
omorrow.

To inspire allows each individual to grown in greater
Knowledge and discover new possibilities.

To inspire yells from every living being, sayings go forth
and achieve great things.

To inspire breaks hold of past failures
and disappointments.

To inspire is the ability to look over one's life and pass
On life lessons learned from experience.

To inspire is who you are women.
Keep inspiring, keep teaching, keep preaching and
keep reaching for your destiny.

Scripture Reading

Psalms 27:14 HCSB

Wait for the LORD; be courageous and let your heart be strong. Wait for the LORD

Prayer

Lord, I pray that from every situation and opportunities that come my way grant me the ability to grasp hold on the knowledge you have for me to learn.

Provide me with strength, intelligence and courage to pass on this knowledge to other individuals so that they become inspire to want more from life. Allow your holy spirit to dwell within me to speak words of life to bring forth life.

Help me to stay in tune with you so that your love and kindness will inspire someone else to show forth your love and kindness.

Don't allow the cares of this world to transcend the purity and beauty of creative to not develop. Strengthen me so that, I will bring forth every creative gift to be used to inspire others to use their creative gifts as well.

In Jesus name Amen.

Thank You!

I would like to personally thank you for purchasing this book. My prayer for you the reader is that one poem, one scripture, or one prayer has enlightened and inspired you to become a better you.

I pray that you will be delivered, healed and set free so you are able to enjoy this beautiful gift called LIFE! No, everything will not be perfect or go according to your plan but trust and know that you are an overcomer in the sight of God.

When the stumbling blocks of life's situations come your way remember to speak **Words of Life** *that uplift and encourage your soul to soar. Never forget to read God's Word and pray because then and only then will true change come.*

Shalom,

Evangelist LaKeisha M. Hall

Jesus Welcomes YOU!

It is God's will that no man should perish **II Peter 3:9**, but that all men should be saved and come to the knowledge of Christ. If you are someone who is not saved today, just say this prayer wherever you are and the Lord Jesus Christ will come into your heart today.

Say Lord Jesus, come into my heart, and forgive me for **ALL** of my sins. I believe that Jesus died for my sins and arose with all power in His hands. I repent and change my mind **TODAY** about former ways. **SAVE ME**, and restore my soul back to you through your son Jesus Christ. I make a **CONCIOUS DECISION** to follow You Lord, and to live a life that is pleasing in your sight. Thank you Lord for saving me!

Romans 10:9 states "That if thou confess with thy mouth the Lord Jesus, and shalt believe in thine heart that God hath risen from the dead, thou shalt be saved."

It is my privilege to welcome you into the Body of Christ, and it is important that you begin to surround yourself with the things and people of God that you may grow in Christ Jesus effectively. It is my earnest prayer that God will lead you, to a Bible believing church, so that you may be strengthened in your new walk with Him.

WELCOME TO THE KINGDOM FAMILY!

About The Author

Evangelist LaKeisha M. Hall is a Philadelphia, PA native who is loved and regarded by many as a powerful intercessor. As a licensed and ordained Evangelist since 2007, she has preached the gospel with power and authority leading many souls to Christ.

In May 2004, Evangelist Hall earned her Bachelor of Science degree in Business Management, and will pursue her Master's degree. She currently resides in Los Angeles, California where she is attends West Angeles Cathedral under the leadership of Bishop Charles E. Blake.

For Additional Information & Speaking Requests

LMH ENTERPRISES, LLC

POST OFFICE BOX 481041

LOS ANGELES, CA 90048

213.538.8999

WWW.LMHENTERPRISE.ORG

SPEAKWORDSOFLIFE2@GMAIL.COM

Words of Life

Speak It!!!

Believe It!!!

Own It!!!

Do It!!!

Notes

Notes

Notes

www.ingramcontent.com/pod-product-compliance
Lightning Source LLC
LaVergne TN
LVHW021515080426
835509LV00018B/2521